Celine Dion Q

101 Questions To Test Yc
Of This Incredibly Successful Musician

By Colin Carter

Celine Dion Quiz

This book contains one hundred and one informative and entertaining trivia questions with multiple choice answers. With 101 questions, some easy, some more demanding, this entertaining book will really test your knowledge of Celine Dion.

You will be quizzed on a wide range of topics associated with Celine Dion for you to test yourself; with questions on her early days, songs, lyrics, achievements, awards and much more, guaranteeing you a truly fun, educational experience.

This quiz book will provide entertainment for fans of all ages and will certainly test your knowledge of this world-famous musician. The book is packed with information and is a must-have for all true Celine Dion fans, wherever you live in the world.

Published by Glowworm Press
glowwormpress.com

Disclaimer

All Rights Reserved. No part of this publication may be reproduced, distributed, or transmitted in any form or by any means, including photocopying, without the written permission of the publisher; with the exception of reviews written for a blog, website, magazine or newspaper and certain other non-commercial uses permitted by copyright law. Product names referred to within this publication are the property of their respective trademark holders. This book is unofficial and is not authorized by the aforementioned interests. This book is licensed for your personal enjoyment only. The image on the cover of this book is either the property of the author/publisher or is used under appropriate licenses or agreements. Any queries please email support@glowwormpress.com

ACKNOWLEDGEMENTS

My niece Cheryl simply adores Celine Dion.

As a writer, I thought I would write a book on Celine Dion for her to test herself and to see how much she really knows about the legend that is Celine.

She told me that she was not alone, and that Celine Dion had millions of fans and that I should write the book for every one of them, not just her.

So I did! This book is for all you wonderful Celine Dion fans – wherever you live in the world.

I do hope you enjoy it.

Colin Carter

OK, Let's get started with the first set of questions.

Q1. When was Celine Dion born?
A. 1967
B. 1968
C. 1969
D. 1970

Q2. What star sign is Celine?
A. Aries
B. Cancer
C. Leo
D. Pisces

Q3. Where was she born?
A. Charlemagne
B. Montreal
C. Quebec City
D. Trois-Rivières

Q4. What is her middle name?
A. Claudette
B. Marie

C. Simone

D. Therese

Q5. How many siblings does she have?

A. 12

B. 13

C. 14

D. 15

Q6. What is the name of Celine's husband?

A. Jean Charbonneau

B. Michel Dion

C. René Angélil

D. Sylvain Dion

Q7. How old was Celine when she first met her husband?

A. 12

B. 17

C. 22

D. 27

Q8. When did they marry?

A. 1990

B. 1992

C. 1994

D. 1996

Q9. Where did they marry?

A. Las Vegas

B. Montreal

C. Paris

D. Quebec City

Q10. What is the name of Celine's first child?

A. Charles

B. René-Charles

C. Simon

D. Thomas

Here are the answers to the first set of questions.

A1. Celine Dion was born on March 30, 1968.

A2. Celine is an Aries. Aries individuals are known for their fiery nature and bold creativity, which aligns with Celine Dion's personality and artistic flair.

A3. Celine was born in Charlemagne, Quebec, Canada.

A4. Celine's full name is Celine Marie Claudette Dion. The name "Marie" is part of her given name but is not used as a middle name in the traditional sense.

A5. Celine is the youngest of 14 children, so she has 13 siblings.

A6. Celine's husband is her long-term manager, René Angélil.

A7. Celine met René for the first time in 1980 when he was 38 and she was just 12 years old.

A8. Celine and René married in 1994.

A9. Celine and René married at the Notre-Dame Basilica in Montreal, Quebec, Canada.

A10. Celine's first child is named René-Charles Angélil. He was born on January 25, 2001.

Here are the next set of questions.

Q11. How many children does Celine have?
A. 1
B. 2
C. 3
D. 4

Q12. Where did Celine grow up?
A. Charlemagne, Quebec
B. Montreal, Quebec
C. Quebec City, Quebec
D. Sherbrooke, Quebec

Q13. What was her first job?
A. Bakery worker
B. Factory worker
C. Singer
D. Waitress

Q14. What is the name of Celine's family restaurant?
A. Dion's Palace
B. La Bonne Saison
C. Le Vieux Baril

D. Thérèse's Bistro

Q15. Which musical instrument did she first learn to play?
A. Drums
B. Guitar
C. Piano
D. Violin

Q16. What was the name of her first band?
A. Les Baronets
B. Les Dion's
C. Les Idoles
D. Les Musiciens

Q17. What color eyes does she have?
A. Blue
B. Brown
C. Green
D. Hazel

Q18. What color hair does she have?
A. Black
B. Blonde
C. Brown

D. Red

Q19. How tall is she?
A. 5' 5"
B. 5' 7"
C. 5' 9"
D. 5' 11"

Q20. What is her nickname?
A. Celine the Queen
B. Diva Dion
C. The French Songbird
D. The Powerhouse

Here is the latest block of answers.

A11. Celine as three children. She and her late husband, René Angélil, had a total of three children: René-Charles and twins Eddy and Nelson.

A12. Celine grew up in Charlemagne, a small town in Quebec, Canada.

A13. Celine's first job was singing in her family's piano bar. As a child, she sang in her family's nightclub, which was managed by her parents.

A14. Celine's parents owned Le Vieux Baril, a small piano bar.

A15. Celine first learned to play the piano. She began learning the piano at a young age, which helped her develop her musical skills and contribute to her early performances.

A16. Celine's first band was Les Baronets. She performed with them during her early years in Quebec.

A17. Celine has blue eyes.

A18. Celine has brown hair.

A19. Celine is 5 feet 9 inches tall.

A20. Celine is often called "The French Songbird" due to her remarkable talent in singing French-language songs. This nickname reflects her exceptional ability and success in performing French music, especially in her early career when she gained fame in the Francophone world before becoming a global superstar.

Here are the next set of questions.

Q21. What is the name of Celine's French-language album released in 1995?

A. D'eux

B. Encore un soir

C. Ma famille

D. S'il suffisait d'aimer

Q22. What is the name of Celine's first English album?

A. A New Day Has Come

B. Dion Chante Plamondon

C. Incognito

D. Unison

Q23. When was this debut album released?

A. 1989

B. 1990

C. 1991

D. 1992

Q24. What was the first single Celine ever released?

A. "D'amour ou d'amitié"

B. "Falling into You"

C. "The Power of Love"

D. "Where Does My Heart Beat Now"

Q25. What is the name of Celine's second English album?

A. A New Day Has Come

B. Celine Dion

C. Falling into You

D. Let's Talk About Love

Q26. What is the name of Celine's third English album?

A. All the Way... A Decade of Song

B. Incognito

C. Taking Chances

D. The Color of My Love

Q27. When did Celine first reach the top of the UK singles chart?

A. 1992

B. 1994

C. 1996

D. 1998

Q28. When did Celine first reach the top of the US singles chart?

A. 1991

B. 1992

C. 1993

D. 1994

Q29. Which was Celine's first number one album in the UK?

A. A New Day Has Come

B. D'eux

C. Let's Talk About Love

D. The Color of My Love

Q30. Which was Celine's first number one album in the US?

A. All the Way... A Decade of Song

B. Falling into You

C. These Are Special Times

D. Unison

Here is the latest block of answers.

A21. Celine released the French-language album D'eux in 1995. It was highly praised and marked a significant milestone in her French music career.

A22. Celine's first English album is Unison. It marked her debut in the English-language market.

A23. Celine's debut English-language album, Unison, was released in 1990.

A24. Celine's first single was "Where Does My Heart Beat Now," which helped her gain recognition in the English-speaking world.

Λ25. Celine's second English-language album, Celine Dion, was released in March 1992. This album is considered one of Céline's most significant works, featuring tracks from renowned songwriters like Diane Warren.

A26. Celine's third album is The Color of My Love, released in 1993.

A27. Celine first reached the top of the UK singles chart with "Think Twice" in 1994.

A28. Celine reached the top of the US singles chart for the first time with "The Power of Love" in 1993.

A29. Celine's first number one album in the UK was "The Colour of My Love."

A30. Celine's first number one album in the US was "Falling into You."

OK, let's have some music video related questions.

Q31. Who directed the music video for the song "My Heart Will Go On"?
A. David Fincher
B. James Cameron
C. Jean-Baptiste Mondino
D. Paul McGuigan

Q32. In which music video does Celine walk through a desert-like setting?
A. "If You Ask Me To"
B. "I'm Your Angel"
C. "Taking Chances"
D. "That's the Way It Is"

Q33. What is the setting of the music video for "The Power of Love"?
A. A desert landscape
B. A futuristic city
C. A grand concert hall
D. A luxurious mansion

Q34. In which music video does Celine perform on a rooftop with a city skyline in the background?

A. "A New Day Has Come"

B. "I'm Alive"

C. "Immortality"

D. "Incredible"

Q35. In which music video does Celine appear in a futuristic outfit, set in a robot research facility with film clips playing on screens in the background?

A. "Beauty And The Beast"

B. "That's the Way It Is"

C. "The Power of Love"

D. "Then You Look at Me"

Q36. Which music video features Celine performing at a county fair with a lively, festive atmosphere?

A. "I Drove All Night"

B. "If That's What It Takes"

C. "Love Can Move Mountains"

D. "Sous le vent "

Q37. In which music video does Celine perform a duet with Andrea Bocelli?
A. "All the Way"
B. "Beauty and the Beast"
C. "The Prayer"
D. "To Love You More"

Q38. Which music video was filmed at a castle and in a studio in Prague?
A. "A New Day Has Come"
B. "Falling into You"
C. "It's All Coming Back to Me Now"
D. "My Heart Will Go On"

Q39. In which music video did Celine and Peabo Bryson's recording session get combined with scenes from a classic fairy-tale film?
A. "Beauty and the Beast"
B. "Falling into You"
C. "My Heart Will Go On"
D. "The Power of Love"

Q40. In which music video does Celine walk through a graveyard and later appear as a ghost in a mansion?

A. "All By Myself"

B. "Because You Loved Me"

C. "Immortality"

D. "Love Me Back To Life"

Here are the answers to the music video questions.

A31. James Cameron directed the music video for "My Heart Will Go On," which was also the theme song for his blockbuster film Titanic.

A32. Celine walks through a desert-like setting in the music video for "Taking Chances." The barren, expansive landscape serves as a metaphor for personal strength and resilience, reflecting the song's themes of risk and adventure.

A33. The music video for "The Power of Love" is set in a luxurious mansion, with a dramatic and opulent atmosphere. The lavish setting enhances the song's themes of deep, enduring love and emotional richness.

A34. Celine performs on a rooftop overlooking Los Angeles in the music video for "Incredible." The video also features real-life talents and a giraffe wandering through the city, adding a unique and surreal element to the visuals.

A35. Celine appears in a futuristic outfit in the music video for "Then You Look at Me." The video is set in a robot research facility and features clips from the film Bicentennial Man displayed on screens in the background.

A36. Celine's music video for "Love Can Move Mountains" features her performing at a county fair. The video captures a lively, festive atmosphere, with Celine mingling with people who are rollerblading, playing basketball, or walking, enhancing the song's upbeat and energetic vibe.

A37. Celine performs a duet with Andrea Bocelli in the music video for "The Prayer."

A38. The music video for "It's All Coming Back to Me Now" was filmed at Castle Ploskovice and Barandov Studios in Prague, Czech Republic. The video features dramatic, theatrical settings, including the historical castle and studio locations.

A39. The music video for "Beauty and the Beast" features Celine and Peabo Bryson's recording session at The Power Station, which was combined with scenes from a classic fairy-tale film of the same title.

A40. The music video for "Immortality" features Celine walking through a graveyard and later appearing as a ghost in a mansion. The video, which deals with themes of love, loss, and reincarnation, also includes appearances by The Bee Gees as ghosts.

Let's have some lyrics related questions.

Q41. Which song begins with the lyrics "I was waiting for so long, For a miracle to come"?
A. "A New Day Has Come"
B. "All By Myself"
C. "I'm Alive"
D. "That's The Way It Is"

Q42. Which song has the opening lyrics "Take me back into the arms I love, need me like you did before"?
A. "Because You Loved Me"
B. "Falling into You"
C. "My Heart Will Go On"
D. "To Love You More"

Q43. Which song opens with "Every night in my dreams, I see you, I feel you"?
A. "Beauty and the Beast"
B. "I'm Your Angel"
C. "My Heart Will Go On"
D. "Think Twice"

Q44. Which song has the opening lyrics "The whispers in the morning of lovers sleeping tight"?
A. "Falling into You"
B. "It's All Coming Back to Me Now"
C. "Taking Chances"
D. "The Power of Love"

Q45. What song begins with "I had to escape, The city was sticky and cruel"?
A. "All By Myself"
B. "I Drove All Night"
C. "Love Can Move Mountains"
D. "That's The Way It Is"

Q46. Which song starts with "There were nights when the wind was so cold that my body froze in bed"?
A. "Beauty And The Beast"
B. "Falling into You"
C. "I'm Alive"
D. "It's All Coming Back to Me Now"

Q47. Which song features the opening lyrics "Don't think I can't feel that there's something wrong"?
A. "I'm Alive"
B. "Love Can Move Mountains"
C. "Taking Chances"
D. "Think Twice"

Q48. Which song begins with "For all those times you stood by me, for all the truth that you made me see"?
A. "Because You Loved Me"
B. "Falling into You"
C. "I'm Your Angel"
D. "The Prayer"

Q49. What song begins with the line "I can read your mind, and I know your story?
A. "Ave Maria"
B. "I'm Alive"
C. "I Love You"
D. "That's The Way It Is"

Q50. What song begins with the lyrics "When I was young, I never needed anyone"?

A. "All By Myself"

B. "Beauty and the Beast"

C. "I'm Your Angel"

D. "Love Can Move Mountains"

Here are the answers to the lyrics questions.

A41. The lyrics "I was waiting for so long, For a miracle to come" are from "A New Day Has Come."

A42. The song with the opening lyrics "Take me back into the arms I love, need me like you did before" is "To Love You More."

A43. "My Heart Will Go On" opens with the lyrics "Every night in my dreams, I see you, I feel you."

A44. The lyrics "The whispers in the morning of lovers sleeping tight" are from "The Power of Love."

A45. The song with the opening lyrics "I had to escape, The city was sticky and cruel" is "I Drove All Night."

A46. The song with the opening lyrics "There were nights when the wind was so cold that my body froze in bed" is "It's All Coming Back to Me Now."

A47. The lyrics "Don't think I can't feel that there's something wrong" are from "Think Twice."

A48. The lyrics "For all those times you stood by me, for all the truth that you made me see" are from "Because You Loved Me."

A49. The lyrics "I can read your mind, and I know your story" are from "That's The Way It Is."

A50. The opening lyrics "When I was young, I never needed anyone" are from "All By Myself."

Now let's have some song collaboration questions.

Q51. Which producer is credited with producing Celine's album "Falling into You"?
A. David Foster
B. Jean-Jacques Goldman
C. Max Martin
D. Ric Wake

Q52. Who did Celine collaborate with for the song "I'm Your Angel"?
A. Barbra Streisand
B. Bryan Adams
C. Michael Bolton
D. R. Kelly

Q53. Who did Celine duet with on the song "The Prayer"?
A. Andrea Bocelli
B. Michael Bolton
C. Peabo Bryson
D. Whitney Houston

Q54. On which song did Celine perform a duet with Barbra Streisand?

A. "No More Tears (Enough Is Enough)"

B. "Tell Him"

C. "The Way We Were"

D. "Woman in Love"

Q55. Who did Celine perform a duet with in "Beauty and the Beast"?

A. Andrea Bocelli

B. Josh Groban

C. Luciano Pavarotti

D. Peabo Bryson

Q56. Which artist did Celine collaborate with on the song "When I Fall in Love"?

A. Andrea Bocelli

B. Clive Griffin

C. Josh Groban

D. Michael Bolton

Q57. Who joined Celine on the song "Incredible"?

A. Andrea Bocelli

B. David Foster

C. Michael Bublé
D. Ne-Yo

Q58. Celine sang "Sous le vent" as a duet with which French-Canadian singer?
A. Garou
B. Jean-Jacques Goldman
C. Lara Fabian
D. Patrick Fiori

Q59. Which song did Celine perform a duet with Frank Sinatra, although Frank had passed away?
A. "All the Way"
B. "Come Fly with Me"
C. "The Way You Look Tonight"
D. "Strangers in the Night"

Q60. Which artist joined Celine to perform "To Love You More" during live events in 1997, including the Juno Awards and a Japanese television show?
A. André Rieu
B. David Foster
C. Taro Hakase

D. Yanni

Here are the answers to the latest questions.

A51. Jean-Jacques Goldman is credited with producing Celine's best-selling album "Falling into You." His involvement was a key factor in the album's success.

A52. Celine collaborated with R. Kelly for the song "I'm Your Angel," which became a popular duet and was featured on her album "These Are Special Times."

A53. Celine was joined by Andrea Bocelli for the track "The Prayer," a powerful duet that has been widely acclaimed.

A54. Celine and Barbra Streisand performed a duet on the song "Tell Him", which showcases their powerful vocal collaboration.

A55. In the song "Beauty and the Beast," Celine performed a memorable duet with Peabo Bryson, creating an iconic soundtrack for the Disney film.

A56. Celine's duet for "When I Fall in Love" was performed with Clive Griffin. The song was featured on the soundtrack for the film Sleepless in Seattle.

A57. Celine performed the song "Incredible" with Ne-Yo, adding a modern touch to her discography.

A58. Celine sang "Sous le vent" as a duet with Garou, blending their vocals in this emotional and heartfelt French song.

A59. Celine's duet with Frank Sinatra is on the song "All the Way." Since Sinatra had passed away before the recording, Celine's vocals were combined digitally with Sinatra's original track from 1957, creating a unique blend of their voices.

A60. Celine performed "To Love You More" with Taro Hakase, a renowned violinist, at both the Juno Awards and on the Japanese television show Music Fair in 1997.

Here are some album-related questions.

Q61. Which album features the song "It's All Coming Back to Me Now"?
A. A New Day Has Come
B. Falling into You
C. Let's Talk About Love
D. One Heart

Q62. Which album features "Where Does My Heart Beat Now?
A. À l'Olympia
B. Courage
C. Taking Chances
D. Unison

Q63. Which album features "Stand by Your Side"?
A. Au Coeur du Stade
B. Incognito
C. One Heart
D. S'il Suffisait d'aimer

Q64. Which album features "Immortality"?
A. A New Day Has Come

B. D'eux

B. Let's Talk About Love

C. Sans attendre

Q65. Which album features the song "Happy Christmas! (War is Over)"?

A. Celine Dion

B. Miracle

C. Taking Chances

D. These Are Special Times

Q66. Which album features "Beautiful Boy (Darling Boy)"?

A. Courage

B. Falling into You

C. Incognito

D. Miracle

Q67. Which album includes the track "Only One Road"?

A. A New Day Has Come

B. Celine Dion

C. Loved Me Back To Life

D. The Colour of My Love

Q68. Which album features the song "Elle"?
A. C'est pour toi
B. Chants et contes de Noel
C. D'elles
D. Tellement j'ai d'amour

Q69. From which album is the song "I Love You Goodbye"?
A. A New Day Has Come
B. Celine Dion
C. Falling Into You
D. Taking Chances

Q70. Which album features the song "Hello Mister Sam?"
A. I Am: Celine Dion
B. La Voix du bon Dieu
C. Les Chemins de ma maison
D. Melanie

Here are the latest answers.

A61. "It's All Coming Back to Me Now" is featured on the album "Falling into You." This song, a dramatic and powerful ballad, was one of the standout tracks on the album, showcasing Celine's emotive vocal performance.

A62. "Where Does My Heart Beat Now" is featured on the album "Unison." This was one of Celine's first major hits in the English-speaking world and helped establish her international career.

A63. "Stand by Your Side" is featured on the English studio album "One Heart". This moving ballad was released as a promotional single in the US.

A64. "Immortality," is featured on the album "Let's Talk About Love," released in 1997. The song showcases Celine's ability to deliver emotional performances alongside The Bee Gees.

A65. "Happy Christmas! (War is Over)" is featured on the album "These Are Special Times," released in 1998. This album is a holiday-themed collection that includes both traditional and original Christmas songs.

A66. "Beautiful Boy (Darling Boy)" is featured on the album "Miracle", released in 2004. This song is part of an album inspired by the theme of motherhood.

A67. Only One Road" is from the album, "The Colour of My Love", released in 1993. This song is one of the notable tracks on an album that features a mix of pop and adult contemporary styles.

A68. "Elle" is featured on the album "D'elles," released in 2007. This album focuses on female perspectives and includes tracks that highlight Celine's deep connection with the material.

A69. "I Love You Goodbye" is from the album, "Celine Dion", released in 1992. The song portrays a woman who, despite her deep love, decides to leave her partner believing her departure is in his best interest.

A70. "Hello Mister Sam" is featured on the album "Les Chemins de ma maison," released in 1995. This album includes a variety of French-language tracks and reflects Celine's work in her native language.

Here is the next set of questions.

Q71. What is Celine's vocal range classified as?
A. Alto
B. Mezzo-soprano
C. Soprano
D. Tenor

Q72. What title is often used to describe Celine due to her powerful singing style?
A. Diva of Soul
B. Empress of Pop
C. Queen of Power Ballads
D. Queen of Rock

Q73. What was Celine's first film?
A. Beauty and the Beast
B. Love Again
C. The Power of Love
D. Up Close and Personal

Q74. Which Olympics opening ceremony did Celine first perform at?
A. Atlanta 1996
B. Sydney 2000

C. Beijing 2008
D. London 2012

Q75. What was the title of Celine's first Las Vegas residency?
A) A New Day…
B) Celine in Vegas
C) Las Vegas Dreams
D) The Best of Celine Dion

Q76. What was the name of Celine's second Las Vegas residency?
A) Celine
B) Celine in Vegas
C) Celine: The Show Must Go On
D) Celine: Through the Eyes of the World

Q77. What was the name of Celine's first major tour in 1994?
A) Falling Into You Around the World Tour
B) Let's Talk About Love Tour
C) Taking Chances World Tour
D) The Colour of My Love Tour

Q78. What was the name of Celine's tour that began in 2008?

A) Celine Dion Live

B) Courage World Tour

C) Let's Talk About Love Tour

D) The Taking Chances World Tour

Q79. How many Golden Globe Awards has Celine won?

A) 1

B) 2

C) 3

D) 4

Q80. Which year did Celine perform at the Olympic opening ceremony in Paris?

A) 2004

B) 2016

C) 2020

D) 2024

Here is the latest set of answers.

A71. Celine's vocal range is classified as mezzo-soprano, with a strong soprano tessitura but less comfort in lower octaves, fitting the mezzo-soprano classification.

A72. Celine is widely known as the Queen of Power Ballads for her remarkable ability to deliver emotional and powerful vocal performances.

A73. Celine's first film is Love Again, released in 2023. In this romantic comedy, she made her acting debut as a fictionalized version of herself, marking a significant step into acting despite her prior contributions to film soundtracks.

A74. Celine first performed at an Olympics opening ceremony at the games in 1996 in Atlanta, where she sang "The Power of the Dream," celebrating the spirit of the games.

A75. Celine's first Las Vegas residency was titled A New Day..... It ran during 2007 at the

Colosseum at Caesar's Palace and is still one of the highest grossing residencies in history.

A76. Celine's second Las Vegas residency was titled Celine. It began in 2011 and continued until 2019, featuring a mix of her greatest hits and new material. It is widely reported she was paid half a million dollars per performance.

A77. Celine's first major tour, "The Colour of My Love Tour," was in support of her 1993 album The Colour of My Love, and it ran from 1994 to 1995.

A78. In 2008, Celine embarked on "The Taking Chances World Tour" to support her album Taking Chances, marking her first worldwide tour in nine years.

A79. Celine has won 2 Golden Globe Awards for Best Original Song: one in 1998 for "My Heart Will Go On" and another in 1999 for "The Prayer."

A80. Celine performed at the opening ceremony of the 2024 Summer Olympics in Paris. She delivered a moving rendition of

"L'Hymne à l'amour" by Édith Piaf from the Eiffel Tower, marking her first performance since announcing her diagnosis with stiff-person syndrome in 2022.

Here is another set of lyrics-related questions.

Q81. In which song would you find the lyrics "I'm your lady, and you are my man"?
A. "If You Asked Me To"
B. "I'm Alive"
C. "My Heart Will Go On"
D. "The Power of Love"

Q82. Which song features the lyrics "You were my strength when I was weak, you were my voice when I couldn't speak"?
A. "All By Myself"
B. "Because You Loved Me"
C. "The Prayer"
D. "To Love You More"

Q83. In which song do the lyrics "Love can touch us one time and last for a lifetime" appear?
A. "A New Day Has Come"
B. "Immortality"
C. "Love Can Move Mountains"
D. "My Heart Will Go On"

Q84. Which song contains the lyrics "There were nights of endless pleasure, it was more than any laws allow"?
A. "It's All Coming Back to Me Now"
B. "Just Walk Away"
C. "Tell Him"
D. "That's the Way It Is"

Q85. In which song would you find the lyrics "Somehow ever since I've been around you, can't go back to being on my own"?
A. "All By Myself"
B. "I Drove All Night"
C. "If You Ask Me To"
D. "To Love You More"

Q86. Which song features the lyrics "Whole world is watching us now, it's a little intimidating"?
A. "Immortality"
B. "Incredible"
C. "Treat Her Like A Lady"
D. "When I Fall In Love"

Q87. In which song would you find the lyrics "I'm the one who'll stay, when she walks away, and you know I'll be standing here still"?
A. "Beauty and the Beast"
B. "Encore un soir"
C. "Falling into You"
D. "To Love You More"

Q88. Which song contains the lyrics "When you want it the most, there's no easy way out"?
A. "A New Day Has Come"
B. "Ashes"
C. "I'm Alive"
D. "That's the Way It Is"

Q89. In which song would you find the lyrics "And I must follow on the road that lies ahead, and I won't let my heart control my head"?
A. "Ave Maria"
B. "Have You Ever Been In Love"
C. "Immortality"
D. "I Surrender"

Q90. Which song contains the lyrics "When you call on me, when I hear you breathe"?

A. "I'm Alive"

B. "Lying Down"

C. "Taking Chances"

D. "The Prayer"

Here are the latest set of answers.

A81. The lyrics "I'm your lady, and you are my man" are from the song "The Power of Love," one of Celine's biggest hits, showcasing her powerful vocals.

A82. The lyrics "You were my strength when I was weak, you were my voice when I couldn't speak" are from "Because You Loved Me," a ballad dedicated to unconditional love and gratitude, and one of her most beloved songs.

A83. The lyrics "Love can touch us one time and last for a lifetime" are from "My Heart Will Go On," the iconic song from the film Titanic.

A84. The lyrics "There were nights of endless pleasure, it was more than any laws allow" come from "It's All Coming Back to Me Now," a powerful, dramatic ballad that became a signature hit for Celine.

A85. The lyrics "Somehow ever since I've been around you, can't go back to being on my own" are from the song "If You Ask Me To," which reflects the deep emotional connection and dependency formed with a loved one.

A86. The lyrics "Whole world is watching us now, it's a little intimidating" are from the song "Incredible." These powerful lyrics speak to the excitement and pressure of achieving something extraordinary in the spotlight.

A87. The lyrics "I'm the one who'll stay, when she walks away, and you know I'll be standing here still" are from the song "To Love You More." The song expresses a deep and unwavering commitment for a loved one.

A88. The lyrics "When you want it the most, there's no easy way out" are from "That's the Way It Is," an empowering song about resilience and determination.

A89. The lyrics "And I must follow on the road that lies ahead, and I won't let my heart control my head" are from the song "Immortality." The song conveys a message of resilience and determination in pursuing one's path.

A90. The lyrics "When you call on me, when I hear you breathe" are from "I'm Alive," an uplifting and energetic track celebrating life and love.

OK, here goes with the final set of questions.

Q91. How many Grammy Awards has Celine won?

A) 5

B) 6

C) 7

D) 8

Q92. For which song did Celine win her first Grammy Award?

A. "Beauty and the Beast"

B. "Because You Loved Me"

C. "My Heart Will Go On"

D. "The Power of Love"

Q93. How many Grammy Awards did Celine win for her song "My Heart Will Go On"?

A. 2

B. 3

C. 4

D. 5

Q94. Which song earned Celine the Grammy Award for Best Female Pop Vocal Performance in 1997?

A. "All By Myself"

B. "Because You Loved Me"

C. "My Heart Will Go On"

D. "The Power of Love"

Q95. For which album did Celine win the World Music Award for Best Selling Female Artist of the Year in 1996?

A. A New Day Has Come

B. Falling into You

C. Let's Talk About Love

D. These Are Special Times

Q96. Which song won Celine an Academy Award for Best Original Song?

A. "Because You Loved Me"

B. "My Heart Will Go On"

C. "The Power of Love"

D. "The Prayer"

Q97. What is Celine's official Instagram account?

A. @celinedion
B. @celinedionofficial
C. @celine.dion
D. @celinedionmusic

Q98. What is Celine's official X (formerly Twitter) account?
A. @celinedion
B. @celinedionmusic
C. @celine.dion
D. @dionceline

Q99. What is Celine's official website?
A. celine.dion.com
B. celinedion.com
C. celinedionmusic.com
D. celineofficial.com

Q100. What is Celine's best-selling single of all time?
A. "Because You Loved Me"
B. "It's All Coming Back to Me Now"
C. "My Heart Will Go On"
D. "The Power of Love"

Q101. What do Celine Dion's fans commonly call themselves?

A. Celine's Angels

B. Celinites

C. Dionites

D. Heartbeats

Here are the answers to the last set of answers.

A91. Celine has won 6 Grammy Awards, recognizing her exceptional talent and contributions to the music industry.

A92. Celine won her first Grammy Award for the song "Beauty and the Beast" in 1993. This duet with Peabo Bryson, featured in Disney's Beauty and the Beast, earned her the award for Best Pop Performance by a Duo or Group with Vocal.

A93. "My Heart Will Go On" earned Celine two Grammy Awards in 1999, including Record of the Year and Best Female Pop Vocal Performance.

A94. Celine won the Grammy Award for Best Female Pop Vocal Performance in 1997 for "Because You Loved Me," a powerful ballad from the Up Close & Personal soundtrack.

A95. Celine won the World Music Award for Best Selling Female Artist of the Year in 1996 for her album "Falling Into You," highlighting its international success.

A96. Celine's "My Heart Will Go On" won the Academy Award for Best Original Song in 1999. It was the theme song for the movie Titanic and became one of her most iconic hits.

A97. Celine's official Instagram account is @celinedion. This account features updates on her music, personal life, and professional achievements.

A98. Celine's official X (formerly Twitter) account is @celinedion. This account provides her followers with news, announcements, and interactions with fans.

A99. Celine's official website is celinedion.com. This site provides comprehensive information about her music, tour dates, and latest news.

A100. Celine's best-selling single of all time is "My Heart Will Go On". This iconic song from the film Titanic has achieved over 20 million physical sales worldwide.

A101. Celine Dion's fans are commonly known as "Heartbeats," a name reflecting their devotion and connection to her music.

That's a great question to finish with.

That's it. I hope you enjoyed this book, and I hope you got most of the answers right. I also hope you learnt some new things about the icon that is Celine Dion!

If you have any comments or if you saw anything wrong, please email celine@glowwormpress.com and we'll get the book updated. We have updated the book thanks to other fans, and we do read every email.

There is just one thing left to do and that's to leave a positive review on Amazon saying what you think of Celine !

Many thanks in advance.

Printed in Great Britain
by Amazon